A 30-minute Summary

of

Ben Carson M.D & Candy Carson's

One Nation

By Instaread Summaries

Please Note

This is an unofficial summary.

Table of Contents

Book Overview

One Nation by Ben Carson and his wife, Candy, is a political guidebook detailing what Carson thinks Americans should do to get the country back on track. Ben Carson, a political conservative, was the keynote speaker at the 2013 National Prayer Breakfast. This book begins with that speech in which he outlined what he believes are the problems that face America today. He also suggested some solutions for these problems and how this country's citizens should work together to bring about these solutions.

Carson expounds further upon his political ideas and philosophies in this book. In order to find solutions to the nation's problems, leaders need to return to morality, common sense, and manners as well as work together to find solutions. Citizens need knowledge and courage to take action toward making the U.S. a better place.

There are several reasons why America is suffering from disunity and decline. Political correctness stifles freedom of speech. Elitists create entitlement programs that encourage dependency and keep the elitists elevated above those who are less fortunate. People, who revise their view of history or forget the past, repeat mistakes instead of learning from them and do not have a proper perspective of current events.

Bigotry with regards to gender, age, religion, race, and sexual orientation is another problem in America that causes disunity. Special interest groups that influence members of Congress, unilateral decisions that do not include both political parties, and dividers that cast doubt on the character of their opponents are all divisive forces that prevent unity among the lawmakers in the U.S.

The ever-increasing, national debt is one reason for this country's decline. Today's leaders need to take care of the federal debt to safeguard the financial future of the next generation. The younger generation of today also needs to be aware of what is happening and make their voices heard.

Americans have options as to how they can work toward uniting the country and getting it back on track. The media, politicians, liberal college professors, businesses, and others can all act as bullies. People can defend themselves against these bullies by fighting back and by gaining their respect.

People need to learn how to disagree with others and still be friendly and cooperative with them. This will help restore unity to the country. Compromise is another necessary element to restore unity to the country. Legislators need to let go of their pride and yield to logic and common sense. They need to serve the people humbly by listening to others and considering their viewpoints and opinions.

Voters need to be educated and informed. Choosing political leaders is a right and a responsibility that can only be done correctly when well informed. Wisdom and knowledge are two different things. Knowledge is the familiarity with facts while wisdom is more like common sense. Wisdom also has to do with knowing how to react appropriately and to prioritize what needs to be done. Americans need to use both wisdom and knowledge to make good decisions.

People need to embrace the mindset that caring for the members of one's family is a basic responsibility. Americans should also have compassion and care for the poor. This is best accomplished by giving them an opportunity to elevate their social status by teaching them the skills they need to find a job to support themselves. On the other side of the issue, people need to humble themselves and take a minimum wage job instead of going on welfare. They may be starting at the bottom, but by continuing to learn and applying themselves, they can soon work their way up to a higher paying job.

America is deeply divided along party lines. This division destroys the country's unity. The Founding Fathers established a vision for America in the Constitution. Americans need to return to that vision and work together to make the country unified again. Proper role models will show the youth of today how to live their lives with humility, ambition, wisdom, and discipline. Although not everyone agrees on the origin of morality, in order to build a successful society, morality should guide the people in the decisions they make.

Americans need to be brave and take action to stand up for the rights that were granted to them in the Constitution. They need to use wisdom and knowledge to choose leaders who care about the people and who have a vision for the nation.

Important People

Ben Carson: Ben Carson is a neurosurgeon, columnist, and conservative author of the political book, *One Nation*. He and his wife set up Carson's Scholarship Fund.

Candy Carson: Candy Carson is Ben Carson's wife and co-author of *One Nation*. She helped him set up the Carson's Scholarship Fund as one way to help make education important in the lives of young people.

Chapter Summaries & Key Takeaways

Preface

Author and neurosurgeon, Ben Carson was invited to give the keynote address at the 2013 National Prayer Breakfast. Carson spoke about numerous problems the U.S. faces and gave his ideas on how some of these problems could be solved. One problem the U.S. faces is that people do not speak their mind because they are afraid of offending others or of being called to task for not being politically correct for the words they choose to use. This fear takes away people's freedom of thought and expression.

Education should be a concern for all. A proper education makes a big difference in people's lives. Carson grew up in a bad environment. He lived with his brother and mother in poverty in a single parent home. Carson's mother wanted her sons to understand how important education could be. She decided to keep the TV turned off most of the time, only allowing her sons to watch two or three television programs a week. She also had her sons read two books from the library each week and write up book reports to give to her about what they read.

Through reading, Carson began to understand that all people have control of their own destinies. People make their own decisions and decide how hard they want to work toward those choices. Carson realized that poverty did not have to be permanent.

Education is important because the American government was designed for educated, well-informed people. Carson and his wife, Candy Carson, set up the Carson Scholarship Fund. Carson's plan was to give scholarships to students who did well academically and who exhibited humanitarian qualities. He wanted to give them the same kind of recognition that superior athletes got. He wanted to make sure they became successful adults and to save them from mediocrity and self-destruction.

The national debt is another problem facing the American nation that needs to be solved. The taxation system needs to be overhauled. People need to pay a certain proportion of their earnings as taxes no matter what income bracket they are in, and the loopholes in the system need to be removed.

Health care is another problem the U.S. needs to solve. Instead of Obamacare, Carson feels that when each person is born, he or she should be given a health savings account and an electronic medical record. Money can then be contributed to this account throughout that person's life, and funds in the account can be passed on to another family member if there is any remaining when that person dies. The government can contribute money to the accounts of those who are indigent. Since people will have a limited amount of money in their accounts, they will learn to be responsible with their funds and will shop around for the best, affordable medical care. They will also be motivated to take better care of their own health.

For all of the problems facing the nation, people of all viewpoints and party affiliations need to put aside their differences and work things out through respectful discussion and compromise until solutions can be found. Only when people work together in unity with the same vision and goals can they start to solve the problems facing the U.S. and make the future better for the young people of today.

Key Takeaways

- In his speech at the 2013 National Prayer Breakfast, neurosurgeon Ben Carson outlined the problems he felt the U.S. faces and suggested some possible solutions to those problems.
- The worst problems facing America today, according to Carson, are: people have lost their freedom of

speech because they are afraid of being accused of not being politically correct, many people are not getting the proper education they need to succeed in the world, the national debt continues to grow unchecked, and a better health care plan needs to be put into place.

- The problems in the U.S. can be solved if people of all viewpoints, no matter what their party affiliation, discussed the issues calmly and rationally and worked together to find a solution.

Chapter 1

To secure the future for the next generation, Americans need to take quick, decisive, and prayerful action. Problems facing the U.S. today include: lack of education, bigotry, elitism, moral issues that have divided the people, and financial issues. The nation's leaders need to return to morality, common sense, and manners in order to work together and find solutions. Individuals should educate themselves and their children, hold their political officials accountable, learn how to compromise, and pray for wisdom.

Bullying seems to be on the rise in the nation's schools. Children are learning to be bullies by watching the adults in their lives. In order to put an end to the bullying problem in the schools, adults need to set a good example by working harder to see things from the other person's perspective, ignoring the rules of political correctness, and engaging in intelligent discussions.

In addition to common sense and manners, people need to be educated. A good education gives a person power. Courage is also required to stand up to secular progressives and other bad influences who want to lead the U.S. away from the values set up by the founding fathers in the Constitution. If individuals take action on their own, collectively they can pass on to the next generation a country they can be proud of.

Key Takeaways

- In order to find solutions to the nation's problems, leaders need to return to morality, common sense, and manners in order to work together and find solutions.
- Children learn bullying by watching adults. Adults need to set a better example for their children by trying to see other people's points of view, ignoring political correctness, and engaging in discussions open to compromise.
- Individuals need knowledge and courage to take action toward making the U.S. a better place.

Part One

Chapter 2

The "political correctness police" (PCP) have established what they consider proper speech guidelines. They have created a list of terms that they deem offensive. This list is an attempt to control the speech of others and it violates the principles of freedom of speech. People who use these words are belittled or mocked. Open communication is the key to solving problems. Political correctness closes down the lines of communication by silencing people. Mature adults should be able to hear an opinion different from their own and still listen with an open mind. They should also be capable of civility in their response.

The best way to respond to the PCP is to communicate in a method and tone that is not reactionary or harsh. Even when under sharp attack, people need to refrain from reacting out of fear or anger. Otherwise, they may just end up discrediting themselves. The greater goal is to have a rational discussion and work together to try and solve problems instead of verbally attacking one another.

Freedom of speech was important to the founders of the U.S., and it should be important to U.S. citizens today. This is why Americans should ignore the PCP who try to silence them. People should stop being hypersensitive and learn to work out differences in a civil manner.

Key Takeaways

- There are terms that are considered offensive and not politically correct. People who use these terms are belittled or mocked by what is known as the political correctness police (PCP).
- Hypersensitivity and accusations of being politically incorrect silences people. It takes away their freedom of speech.
- People should not take what someone says personally. Instead, they need to look at the issue from the other person's point of view and react rationally and kindly when someone says something that is ignorant, mean, or insensitive.

Chapter 3

Elitism used to be measured by wealth alone, but it has come to mean wealth, education, and influence combined with arrogance. The elite are convinced they know what is best for everyone. They think they are wiser than those who believe in God and the Bible. They impose their will upon those who are less fortunate than themselves in a misguided attempt to help them.

Elitists create programs that encourage dependency, such as food stamps and subsidized health care, in the guise of helping them. These types of entitlement programs keep the elitists elevated above those who are less fortunate. Opportunities to teach the less fortunate self-reliance and self-help would improve their situations in life much more than entitlement programs do.

One way the black community can stop depending on help from the elite is to lower the number of babies born out-of-wedlock. Young women need to be taught self-respect and what life is like for a single mother. Most single mothers drop out of school and work minimum wage, dead end jobs, forcing them and their children to live in poverty. One way leaders can help prevent this is to make sure affordable childcare is available in areas where teen pregnancy rates are high so that young mothers can finish their education. This could also be prevented if young women were to develop a better sense of self-esteem and learned to be independent.

Many young black men get entangled in the criminal justice system. This decreases the likelihood they will be successfully employed and increases the chances of them being involved in violence or being imprisoned. Their talents and intellect are being wasted for themselves and for society.

Both men and women need to be taught the basics of economics and finances, and they need to get a good education. People can take back the power that has been taken away from them by elitists if they are properly educated.

Key Takeaways

- Elitists create programs that encourage dependency, such as food stamps and subsidized health care, under the pretense of helping the poor. In reality, these programs keep the poor from being independent.
- Young women need to be taught how difficult it is to be a single mother and how to avoid becoming one. Teen mothers often drop out of school, taking minimum wage, dead end jobs that lead to poverty for them and their children.
- Young men need to be taught how to stay out of trouble and away from the criminal justice system. Instead of finding jobs and being productive citizens, they are involved in violence and often incarcerated.

Chapter 4

People sometimes selectively forget painful memories from the past. They want to distance themselves from failure and embarrassment. This revisionism of history can be a dangerous practice. People rewrite history in their minds in an attempt to get rid of guilt and feel better about themselves. It is better to remember the past and learn from it.

People also rewrite history in order to shine a light on mistakes and wrongdoings of the past. They attempt to portray the U.S. as uncaring and opportunistic and in need of change. The U.S. made mistakes, but it is still one of the kindest superpowers the world has ever known. It is important that the U.S. continues its status as a pinnacle nation because if it loses this status to another country, it will more than likely be replaced by a nation that is less benign.

Historical revisionists sometimes downplay the Christian heritage of America. However, religion was very important in the development of this country. Historically, education was considered a vital part of a child's upbringing and the Bible was used to teach morality in the public school system. The Founding Fathers did not want the church to be in control of public policy or the government to decide religious practices for its people, but they intended for the people to be moral and religious.

People need to be aware of what has happened in the past in order to have a proper perspective of current events. It is because of ignorance that history often repeats itself. With knowledge of the past, people can avoid making the same mistakes. As a pinnacle country, the U.S. has a great responsibility to lead. The events of the day must be kept in the proper historical context in order to evaluate what needs to be done to solve the problems facing the world.

Key Takeaways

- People revise history in their minds in an attempt to get rid of guilt and feel better about themselves. It is better to remember the past and learn from it.
- Historical revisionists sometimes downplay the part Christianity played in America's heritage. The Founding Fathers did not want the church to be in control of public policy or for the government to decide religious practices for its people, but they intended for the people to be moral and religious.
- Events of the past help people keep current events in proper perspective.

Chapter 5

Bigotry happens when people are ignorant and live sheltered lives. When people are not familiar with those in another group, they are more likely to have negative views about them. Bigotry is a problem in America with regards to gender, age, religion, race, and sexual orientation.

Legalized segregation is over, but prejudice and racist bigotry is still a problem today. Blacks and whites still make false assumptions and generalizations about each other. These assumptions are a detriment to race relations. Handouts given to able-bodied people instead of requiring them to work for pay is a form of racism practiced today. These entitlement programs do more harm than good.

Religious bigotry is another problem in the U.S. Although America claims to practice religious tolerance, improvement is still needed in this area. Due to the actions of religious extremists, some people want to shun religion as a whole.

The Christian faith, which is based on the teachings of Jesus Christ, is centered on love, acceptance, and forgiveness. Love of God and the love of neighbors are the two main principles behind Christianity. True Christians leave judging to God and do not try to impose their beliefs on others. Some people have distorted the view of Christianity, however, as being intolerant of other faiths. This has alienated many people to Christianity.

The Constitution says the government should not prevent the expression of anyone's religion. When some people demand the removal of symbols of Christianity, such as crosses, religious statues, manger scenes, and Christmas trees, they are preventing the expression of religion. These people also want to remove references to God from the pledge of allegiance and from U.S. currency. Religious freedom should support these expressions instead of trying to restrict them. Every group should be encouraged to have this freedom of expression. People need to stand up against religious bigotry to keep from losing all religious freedoms.

Although not as bad as it once was, sexism is another problem facing Americans today. Men and women are equally competent. Evaluation of a person's competence for a job should be based on his or her abilities, not on their sex. Both men and women should be treated respectfully. They should work together, allowing both sexes to use their strengths and talents to reach a common goal.

Ageism causes problems for America today, too. Young people often do not have respect for the elderly, and those in older generations often have negative impressions of today's youth. Young people need to look up to and seek out the wisdom of the elderly and be prepared to care for them when it becomes necessary. The older generation needs to remember that they have an obligation to the younger generation and should adopt policies that will ensure prosperity for them.

Bigotry with regard to sexual orientation is another issue facing America. Although gay bashing is lessening, much improvement is still needed toward the acceptance of views that are considered different. Hatred on either side of the issue should not be tolerated. A country that was formed based on the principles of liberty and justice for all needs to live those words in order to remain a strong leader in the world today.

Key Takeaways

- Bigotry with regard to gender, age, religion, race, and sexual orientation continues to be a problem in America today.
- The Constitution says the U.S. government should not prevent the expression of anyone's religion.
- A country that was formed based on the principles of liberty and justice for all needs to live those words in order to remain a strong leader in the world today. People need to look beyond their differences with others in order to make this nation a united one.

Chapter 6

Divisive forces have put a wedge between the two main political parties in America. Instead of working together to solve problems, the two parties now pin the blame for lack of progress on each other. When there is a lack of unity, problems cannot be solved effectively.

There are four tactics used by the dividers: demonization of opponents, holding up someone as a victim of opponents and claiming this will happen to everyone, making sweeping, false statements about their opponents to fool gullible voters, and quoting their opponents out of context. All of these tactics are meant to cast doubt upon their opponents' character.

The government has become too big, taking over all parts of people's lives. People need to fight back to regain their rights. They should practice intelligent voting instead of holding on to blind loyalty to a party platform.

People from all parties need to stop quarreling and seek a true unity. They need to see past the efforts of the dividers. They must be able to have a civil discussion without name calling and bickering.

Key Takeaways

- There are many divisive forces that prevent unity among the lawmakers in the U.S.
- The government has become too big, taking over all parts of people's lives. People need to fight back to regain their rights
- Members of all political parties need to stop quarreling and seek a true unity. They need to see past the efforts of the dividers and be able to have a civil discussion without name calling.

Chapter 7

The U.S.'s national debt is close to $17 trillion, and it could go beyond $20 trillion in the next few years. This debt puts the financial future of generations to come in jeopardy.

Budget cuts can be put in place to repair the national debt, but economic growth is the real answer to the problem. The Constitution's intention was to have a limited government which would not require a lot of money or cause such a debt. Leaders need to carefully analyze the current financial situation and compare it to history in order to recognize errors and get back on the right path.

There is waste in every federal program where cuts can, and should, be made. A certain percentage should be cut from every program with no exceptions. These cuts should be made every year until the federal debt is eliminated.

The next generation needs to pay attention to what is happening in today's government. They need to speak up and encourage the current leaders to solve the problem of the national debt in order to secure their own future.

Key Takeaways

- The national debt is a huge problem that needs to be addressed.

- Leaders need to cut budgets and encourage economic growth in order to get rid of the national debt.
- Today's leaders need to take care of the federal debt to safeguard the financial future of the next generation. The younger generation of today also needs to be aware of what is happening and make their voices heard.

Part Two

Chapter 8

Americans often feel bullied by historical revisionists, bigots, elites, dividers, PCP, and spenders, but it is important that they take action. Bullies can be defeated by standing up to them and by gaining their respect. They can be stopped with calm, mature, and rational action.

The media sometimes acts as a bully. It has the advantage of a regular platform from which it can attack its victims. Social media is one avenue to use in fighting back against media bullies. When a significant number of people are convinced there is a problem, boycotts of the offending media bullies can be held. Members of the media are sensitive to changes in their ratings which can be affected by a boycott.

Political bullies are also sensitive to organized resistance through social media. They do not want to risk losing the support of voters. They will sit up and take notice if organized groups point out their mistakes.

Liberal college professors act as bullies when they teach from a liberal perspective and punish students who have different views. University officials are often liberal as well and, therefore, do not hold the professors to the high standard of fairness. Students must appeal to the university board of trustees in order to fight back against political bias on campus.

Businesses also can be bullies. Collective community action, boycotts, and public demonstrations against them will effectively withhold the financial resources of businesses.

Citizens do not need to hold an armed insurrection to fight back. Some things they can do are: educate their neighbors, have community discussions that include representative officials, circulate petitions, and use social media to influence others. These methods will help them fight back against government that has grown too big and give power back to the people where it belongs.

Sometimes citizens can defeat bullies by gaining their respect. People can do this by refusing to take disrespect and insubordination. People need to remain calm, courteous, and nice when dealing with those who are trying to bully them.

Key Takeaways

- The media, politicians, liberal college professors, businesses, and others can all act as bullies against American citizens.
- People can defend themselves against these bullies by fighting back and by gaining their respect.
- People can fight back against bullies by educating their neighbors, having community discussions that include representative officials, circulating petitions, and using social media to influence others. They can gain the respect of bullies by remaining calm and courteous, refusing to take disrespect and insubordination, educating themselves, and staying informed.

Chapter 9

It is possible to disagree with others and still be friendly and cooperative with them. Americans need to learn this if the country is going to be able to move forward. There are several divisive issues facing the nation currently. They include: abortion, welfare, rising medical costs, and fair taxation. People on both sides of these issues need to practice empathy and try to understand the viewpoints of others.

Both parties should show humility and be willing to listen. Compromise and respect are also necessary. There should be no name-calling. Both parties should focus on the issue at hand and keep in mind the big picture instead of the small details.

The first step is to find the common ground that both parties agree is important. The second step is to determine if anyone might be harmed by the position of either party. The parties should agree not to intentionally hurt others. Last, the parties need to show tolerance, but hold onto core values. The only way compromises can be made and problems solved is if intelligent conversations are held with respect for all.

Key Takeaways

- There are several issues facing the nation currently on which people have strong opposing views. They include: abortion, welfare, rising medical costs, and fair taxation.

- It is possible to disagree with other people and still be friendly and cooperative with them. Americans need to learn this if the country is going to be able to move forward.
- The only way compromises can be made and problems solved is if intelligent conversations are held with respect for all. Both parties should show humility and be willing to listen.

Chapter 10

Compromise seems to be a lost art with both political parties insisting on having things done their way. They do not seem to mind if discussions get stuck in gridlock. Legislators need to put aside their differences and work together systematically to solve differences.

The records are available for people to check if their representatives are working for the people or for special interest groups. Compromises can be found if the legislators are willing to work for them. Problems can be solved only when neither side has a complete victory or suffers a total defeat. Both sides make concessions in order to find a solution. Some of the big issues the U.S. currently faces that require compromise are gay marriage, the national debt, and taxation.

Legislators need to let go of their pride and be willing to yield to logic and common sense. They need to serve the people humbly by listening to others and considering their viewpoints and opinions.

Key Takeaways

- Both political parties in the legislature do not seem to mind if discussions get stuck in gridlock. Compromise should be their goal instead of holding on stubbornly to their ideas.

- Problems can be solved only when neither side has a complete victory or suffers a total defeat. Both sides should make concessions in order to find a solution.
- Some of the big issues the U.S. currently faces that require compromise are gay marriage, the national debt, and taxation. Legislators need to practice humility and learn how to listen to others in order to reach compromises.

Chapter 11

Young people today need to continually increase their knowledge because there is always room for improvement and always more to learn. A voter's choice of political leaders is a right and a responsibility that can only be done correctly when the voter is well informed. Voters need to look past party affiliation to make wise choices in the voting booth.

A lack of education can lead to inaction on the part of the voter. Tens of millions of eligible people did not vote in the last presidential election. Some were frustrated with the political realm. Others felt their vote would not count or would not matter. The choice to not vote makes matters worse because people who do not vote are giving up their rights and power to have a say in the government.

A good education is important because it will affect a person's entire life. Education is the first step toward prosperity, personal fulfillment, and joy. The investment of a little work in a relatively short time by getting an education can pay off in a big way.

Key Takeaways

- Well-informed voters will check the records of their representatives to make sure they are working for the best interests of their constituents. Choosing political leaders is a right and a responsibility that can only be done correctly when well informed.

- Tens of millions of eligible people did not vote in the last presidential election. The choice to not vote makes matters worse because people who do not vote are giving up their rights and power to have a say in government.
- A good education is important because it will affect a person's entire life. Education is the first step towards prosperity, personal fulfillment, and joy.

Chapter 12

Some people think of wisdom and knowledge as being the same things, but they are not. Knowledge is a familiarity with facts and information. A person with a lot of knowledge can do a lot of things. Wisdom helps people prioritize what they should be doing. For the most part, wisdom is the same thing as common sense.

In order to have a health system that functions well, the health of the people needs to be the first priority of a government. In order to bring about reform, the goals must first be defined. These goals include decreasing the rising costs of health care, guaranteeing access to basic healthcare for everyone, restoring a proper balance to the doctor-patient relationship, and putting people back in charge of their own health.

Carson believes that everyone should be given a health savings account (HSA) at birth, as well as an electronic medical record (EMR), such as an electronic chip embedded into a card, which can be shared with a physician or other health care provider. Funds for the HSA could come from the owner of the account, an employer, friends, relatives, and governmental sources. The government would only need to contribute to the accounts of those who are unable earn an income.

This system would put people in charge of their own health, bring down costs, and decrease the bureaucracy problem that is prevalent in healthcare today for both the patient and the provider.

A national tort reform would also be an important part of this plan. The system should also include a way for people to be appropriately and immediately compensated for medical injury. It should be a matter of record which doctors cause these injuries so that patients can choose their physicians wisely. These physicians should also be retrained and disciplinary action taken against them.

One of the main aspects of wisdom is the ability to learn from mistakes. Another sign of wisdom is the ability to prioritize. A proper perspective is what gives a person wisdom. A wise person is aware that he or she does not know everything. Wise people also learn from both the success and failure. Wise people also pray to seek guidance from God, who is the source of all wisdom.

Key Takeaways

- Wisdom and knowledge are two different things. Knowledge is the familiarity with facts while wisdom is more like common sense. Wisdom is the knowledge of how to react appropriately in specific situations and the ability to prioritize what needs to be done.
- A new healthcare program needs to be established that places the control of health care into the hands of the patient, brings down the cost of medical care, and provides basic health care for all. Tort reform as well as immediate and appropriate compensation for medical injury should be a part of this program.

- People who are wise learn from mistakes and successes, and pray for guidance and wisdom from God.

Chapter 13

Many people expect the government to care for elderly or disabled family members instead of doing it themselves. This results in lower quality of care and additional national debt. The U.S. will continue to decline as a nation until this practice is changed. People need to embrace the mindset that caring for the members of their family is a basic responsibility.

Some people must work outside the home in order to make ends meet and cannot care for their elderly parents or disabled family members at home. Others do not have the compassion to care for their own family members. Nursing homes and elder care facilities are a solution for these people.

Adult day care centers are becoming increasingly popular. These centers have created jobs for some and provide a safe environment for those who need it. Many of these centers are operated with little or no assistance from the government. These independent centers should be encouraged.

Americans should have compassion for and care for the poor. This does not mean giving handouts. It does mean giving them an opportunity to elevate their social status by teaching them the skills they need in order to find a job to support themselves. If they can take care of themselves, the government does not need to do it.

Ideally, people helping people will become more commonplace instead of the government helping people. Churches and other charitable organizations can play a part in this movement. The economy will be given a boost if these organizations can give people a hand up rather than a handout.

Those who are capable but who will not take care of themselves should be allowed to experience the consequences of their actions. The government should not be responsible for providing for the needs of all people, especially if these people, by choice, make no effort to provide for themselves.

Key Takeaways

- People need to embrace the mindset that caring for the members of their family is a basic responsibility. Adult day care centers, that are not dependent on the government, provide a good option and safe environment for the care of people whose families must work a full-time job and cannot care for them at home.
- Americans should also have compassion for and care for the poor. This is best accomplished by giving them an opportunity to elevate their social status by teaching them the skills they need to find a job to support themselves.

Part Three

Chapter 14

A society must have a shared vision of its goals in order to progress. The Constitution was designed to protect the rights of the people. It was not set up to protect the rights of the government to rule the people. If Americans live by the principles of the Constitution, their freedoms will be safe.

Lawmakers seem to think they know what is best for the people instead of letting the people decide for themselves. America needs to get back to the original vision for the country that was established by the Constitution. Doing this will help bring down the national debt, get people off of welfare and back to work, and return the U.S. to a position of leadership and respect.

This country is deeply divided along political party lines. Dramatic changes occur whenever power shifts from one party to another. This destroys the country's unity. Many issues create division in America today. Some of them are: belief in God vs. atheism, personal responsibility vs. government dependency, strong international leadership vs. a more laid-back attitude, the right to own guns vs. public safety, and differing viewpoints with regard to social issues such as abortion and gay marriage.

Key Takeaways

- The Founding Fathers established a vision for America in the words of the Constitution. If Americans live by the principles of the Constitution, their freedoms will be safe.
- The US is deeply divided along party lines. Dramatic changes occur whenever power shifts from one party to another which destroys the country's unity.

Chapter 15

Success is not an accident, and it takes more than luck to make it happen. People achieve success because they decide to work for it and make it happen. People need to realize that they do not have to be victims of circumstance, and they do have some control over their destiny. Those who have a vision and set goals are more likely to achieve success. They have a plan and can see what they need to do to stay on track.

Young people need proper role models to inspire them and show them what their lives can be like. Parents and guardians should try to be proper role models for their children as well as guide them to make good choices. Proper role models will inspire the youth of today to live their lives with humility, ambition, wisdom, and discipline. Young people should focus on using their talents to contribute to society.

Key Takeaways

- Success is more than luck. People achieve success because they decide to work for it and make it happen.
- Young people need proper role models to inspire them. Proper role models will show the youth of today how to live their lives with humility, ambition, wisdom, and discipline.

Chapter 16

For a country to be united, most of its citizens must agree on what is right and what is wrong. Historically, most Americans determined right from wrong based on what they learned from the Bible. For the most part, U.S. citizens believed in a Judeo-Christian standard but respected those who had different beliefs. Many now reject the moral standards set forth in the Bible.

A return to those traditions would make some of the divisive social issues of today clearer as far as whether they should be considered right or wrong. Those who believe the Biblical teaching that it is wrong to kill will think that abortion is wrong. Some believe that God disapproves of homosexuality according to how they interpret the Bible. They also say that according to the Bible, marriage between a man and a woman is an institution established by God. The theory of evolution is contradictory to what creationists believe the Bible tells them.

Although not everyone agrees on the origin of morality, it should be obvious that in order to build a successful society, a sense of morality should guide the people in the decisions that they make.

Key Takeaways

- For a country to be united, most of its citizens must agree on what is right and what is wrong.
- Historically, most Americans determined right from wrong based on what they learned from the Bible, but now many reject those moral standards.
- A return to the tradition of using the Bible as a moral compass would make some of the divisive social issues of the day clearer as far as whether they should be considered right or wrong. A sense of morality should guide the people in the decisions they make.

Chapter 17

People can develop courage by thinking about what will happen if they fail to act. They need to figure out what would be the worst thing and the best thing that would happen if they act and if they do not act. Americans need to be brave and take action. They need to stand up for the rights that were granted to them in the Constitution.

Key Takeaways

- Americans need to be brave and take action. They need to stand up for the rights that were granted to them in the Constitution.

Epilogue

American citizens need to get rid of their apathy now and act responsibly in an informed manner to bring back the freedoms that have been taken away from them. They need to use wisdom and knowledge to choose leaders who care about the people and have a vision for the nation. The American people need to work together to help the nation return to greatness.

Key Takeaways

- American citizens need to get rid of their apathy now and act responsibly and in an informed manner to bring back the freedoms that have been taken away from them.
- Americans need to use wisdom and knowledge to choose leaders who care about the people and have a vision for the nation.

A Reader's Perspective

One Nation by Ben and Candy Carson begins with the keynote speech that Ben Carson gave at the 2013 National Prayer Breakfast. In that speech, Carson outlined his view of what problems face America, some of his ideas for solutions to those problems, and how he thinks both the legislators and the citizens of this country are responsible for getting the country back on track by following the vision laid out by the Constitution.

Carson takes the main points from this speech and expounds upon them in One Nation. Although Carson claims that he is not running for office, his message in this book is certainly a political one that could be interpreted as coming from someone who would like to be an elected official.

Ben Carson is a conservative Christian, a columnist, and a retired pediatric neurosurgeon. One Nation is very easy to read and is a book that would appeal to the general population. Carson's ideas on how some of the problems facing the country can be fixed are mostly based on common sense, although some are a bit oversimplified in this book. He does not go into great detail with his solutions as he prefers to stick with the big picture.

Some of Carson's personal opinions on current topics that divide the nation are controversial, and not everyone who reads this book will agree with what he has to say about such topics as homosexuality, gay marriage, abortion, and welfare. Carson realizes this and tries to show both sides of the issues. He does, however, make it very clear where he stands and what he believes.

Carson believes the tax system needs to be overhauled by getting rid of tax loopholes and having everyone taxed proportionately. Instead of Obamacare, he thinks everyone should have a health savings account assigned to them at birth. Contributions to this account could come from several sources. He feels that if everyone had this limited account, they would shop around for the best priced medical care, which would in turn bring down the cost of care. Carson believes that those who are able-bodied and able to hold a job should do so and should not be on welfare. He believes in giving people a hand up instead of a handout. Although his solutions make sense in their simplified form, Carson tends to look at these situations from an everything is black or white point of view. He does not make any allowances for gray areas.

Education is a topic about which Carson feels very strongly. He is an advocate for all citizens receiving the best education they can. He believes that education is the key to individual success. He also believes voters need to be educated so they can make wise choices when electing their political leaders. Carson and his wife, in an effort to help those less fortunate, set up the Carson Scholarship Fund. He wanted academic students to be honored and recognized as much as athletic students. Carson is a shining example of how far a good education can take someone. He grew up in poverty as the child of a single mother. As an adult, Carson became a successful pediatric neurosurgeon. He speaks from experience and his words ring true when he writes about how much a good education can change a person's life.

Carson also writes about how he thinks the nation's leaders and the general population need to work harder toward compromise and unifying the country. Carson believes there is too much name calling and bickering among politicians. He advocates for people to see situations through the eyes of their opponents and to set and work toward common goals through cooperative efforts. This part of Carson's advice makes good sense and probably would help solve some of the problems facing the U.S. if enough leaders and voters followed his advice. Unfortunately, as divided as the country is right now, it seems unlikely that very many will listen to what Carson has to say.

~~~~~~~ END OF SUMMARY~~~~~~~

Made in the USA
Lexington, KY
29 July 2015